Authentic Balti Curry

Restaurant Recipes Revealed

Mohammed Ali Haydor

Edited by

Andy Holmes

Note for Librarians: A cataloguing record for this book is available from Library and Archives
Canada at www.collectionscanada.ca/amicus/index-e.html
ISBN 1-4120-5592-X

*Printed in Victoria, BC, Canada. Printed on paper with minimum 30% recycled fibre. Trafford's print shop
runs on "green energy" from solar, wind and other environmentally-friendly power sources.*

Offices in Canada, USA, Ireland and UK
This book was published *on-demand* in cooperation with Trafford Publishing. On-demand
publishing is a unique process and service of making a book available for retail sale to the
public taking advantage of on-demand manufacturing and Internet marketing. On-demand
publishing includes promotions, retail sales, manufacturing, order fulfilment, accounting and
collecting royalties on behalf of the author.

Book sales for North America and international:
Trafford Publishing, 6E–2333 Government St.,
Victoria, BC v8t 4p4 CANADA
phone 250 383 6864 (toll-free 1 888 232 4444)
fax 250 383 6804; email to orders@trafford.com
Book sales in Europe:
Trafford Publishing (uk) Limited, 9 Park End Street, 2nd Floor
Oxford, UK ox1 1hh UNITED KINGDOM
phone 44 (0)1865 722 113 (local rate 0845 230 9601)
facsimile 44 (0)1865 722 868; info.uk@trafford.com
Order online at:
trafford.com/05-0490

10 9 8 7 6 5 4 3 2 1

Contents

QUICK START!
To begin making curries right now, go to page 11

Cover photograph shows Chicken Korma (double portion) - recipe on page 41

Chapter One

Travelling the world in search of the perfect Balti

We all love a curry. It's been one of Britain's most popular meals for decades. As a restaurant owner, people are constantly asking me how to make the dishes I serve. "Somehow," they say, "No matter what sort of Indian curry cook book I try, it's never the same".

There are hundreds of cookery books on the market but, my customers tell me that they contain dishes which are too elaborate or exotic - when all they want to do is try their hand at making a Balti Lamb Bhuna or Chicken Tikka Masala. Hopefully, I'll change all that in the following pages. But, be warned - preparing restaurant-style curries isn't just a matter of mixing a few spices and throwing in some meat! The preparation stage can take an hour or so, but fans of Indian and Balti cuisine will find it fascinating to see how it all comes together - and your dinner party guests will be pleasantly surprised. Either that or they'll think you've sent out for a take away.

I'm never sure whether to believe the claims in the media that Chicken Tikka Masala is now Britain's favourite meal. Whatever the truth, it is undeniably one of most popular dishes in my restaurant, and therefore has to be included in this book. We'll start with a basic chicken (or whatever meat or vegetable you prefer) Balti - and then get more and more elaborate until we reach that culinary milestone. Chicken Tikka Masala. Also included are recipes for accompaniments and Indian breads.

When talking about the curry culture, it seems to be largely referred to as "Indian" - but that's not strictly true. Yes, there are a lot of top chefs in the UK from India, but in my experience the majority of British curry restaurants belong to people of Bangladeshi origin. Curry can, of course, come from India, Saudi Arabia, Thailand, Bangladesh, and many other countries. When entrepreneurs arrived from across Asia to set up businesses in the UK, a great number were from Bangladesh but it seems that for simplicity's sake, the cuisine was called Indian. And it still is today by many people.

I, myself, am from the Sylhet district of Bangladesh - a rural area in the north. Bangladesh features heavily in my quest to discover the perfect Balti curry. I've travelled extensively during my time as a chef to seek out the authentic curry-making techniques, which have inspired many a Balti-house Bhuna on high streets across the UK.

My search really began when I was a trainee chef in the 1970s - many years before the Balti craze took off. My earliest memory is of a chef from Nepal who I worked with at a busy restaurant at Euston in London. I spent six years during the seventies sharing a kitchen with this man - who I still consider to be the master of the art of tandoori. This is a method of cooking using the "tandoor" - a large clay oven, still used in most curry houses today.

Tandoori cuisine was not a curry as most people would recognise it now, but meats marinated in spices and "baked" to give a very moist, yet spicy, texture. It's still very popular but, overall, tends to come second place to the more widely recognised "meat-in-sauce" type dishes. Tandoori food could be very messy. Meat cooked on the bone would be eaten without knives and forks, meaning finger bowls and hot towels needed to be on constant standby. At the time, this was part of the attraction. Not only was this an exotic dish, it broke the boundaries of eating for many people. Cutlery was simply not necessary. As I'll describe later in this chapter, it makes for more of an authentic culinary experience, as it's just how the food was designed to be eaten.

As curry houses grew in popularity, so did the desire to modernise the curry industry's image. Enter the "Balti" - a food phenomenon that was to take the country by storm. Balti was born in the West Midlands - and Birmingham still claims to be its ancestral home. With the high Asian population, this new way of cooking and serving curries soon grabbed peoples' attention. Many people still maintain that Birmingham is the only place where you can get a genuine Balti. Balti cuisine was - and still is - a stroke of genius; a new type of curry, cooked and served in the same small metal wok, with your choice of naan bread or rice. And the Brummies loved it. In the early nineties there were Balti houses appearing almost on a weekly basis, and the Balti Triangle of Moseley, Balsall Heath and Sparkbrook expanded to become a mass of neon signs and brightly coloured shop fronts along narrow roads. These inevitably became heavily congested with curry-lovers heading to their favourite restaurant, and the area became an instant tourist attraction.

I was intrigued to know how this whole craze came about and, with such variety available, I wanted to know exactly what the source of the Balti was. The only way to find out was to go exploring remote parts of Asia. My first port of call was Nepal.

While staying with friends, I suggested seeing a bit more of the country by getting out into the remote, more desolate areas. It was July and very VERY hot. I found myself taking a drive along a rather dusty road which, all of a sudden, came to an end miles from anywhere. My friend informed me that the only way to go from here was on foot - or by donkey. It's a mountainous part of the world, prone to extremes of temperature. One minute it was very hot - the next, quite the opposite. We met a group of natives who live and work on the hillsides where they gather tree bark to sell at the market. While there, they use the money they've just made to buy food and clothes for their family. It's a simple existence - but that's their daily lifestyle. And it's interrupted only by a spot of cooking.

The way they cook can only be described as magical. They practically create something from nothing. This was my first experience of real Balti cooking - and was one of those life-changing moments that makes you realise just how important the simple things are. Armed with nothing more than a bag of rice from the market and their metal wok (the size of which depends on how many people they're cooking for), they head for the hills. One of the men handed me the wok - or "Balti" - and asked me to wash it in a nearby lake with a small waterfall. While I was doing the washing up, two of the men disappeared but swiftly returned with two freshly killed birds - like pheasants - only much larger. They had no guns or ammunition, and to this day I still have no idea how they managed to hunt these animals. As they headed back with the birds, the women in the group were chopping wood to make a fire, which they started with apparent ease, using a technique involving sticks and dried pieces of bark. After scrabbling around in the nearby forest, the men came back with handfuls of leaves and seeds. This aromatic mixture, from what I could tell, included coriander, thyme, cumin, cardamom, cinnamon and many others. They'd also managed to unearth some potent weeds, which they then smoked during a brief "fag-break" before getting down to the serious business of cooking. With their now-skinned and butchered pheasant, they marinated the meat for a short time in the spices, along with some small onions they'd dug up. Then, after adding a precise amount of water from a nearby stream, the whole mixture was cooked over the fire to make the closest thing to a perfect Balti I have ever tasted. And this is what they do every day. They go to a different place where they know there's a plentiful supply of ingredients and turn it into a kitchen. As for cutlery, there were no knives and forks - leaves quite happily sufficed. The Balti bowl was then rinsed out in the stream, and I was guided back to our vehicle down a long and complex maze of paths. My guide pointed out the various other locations rich in spices, making them regular places for their lunch and dinner gatherings. Although a bit of cliché, the countryside really was their own pantry with everything necessary for the best ever Balti.

Leaving Nepal behind, I went to Pakistan. I flew into Karachi - but had really wanted to go to Dakar, as it was easier to explore the small villages and rural areas from there. Sadly, flights to Dakar were not easy to come by, and there was a three-week waiting list. The fact that I couldn't get to my intended destination ultimately turned out to be beneficial. I booked into a hotel for a couple of days, and during that time got talking to the head chef. I explained that we were in the same profession and that I was on a quest to discover the source and the secrets of genuine Balti cooking. With typical Pakistani hospitality he invited me to spend some time with him in the kitchen and was more than happy to explain, in every detail, just what he was doing. The techniques were very similar to those I'd seen in Bangladesh many years previously, but it was fascinating to see such real high-quality "commercial" cooking on such a large scale.

As a restaurateur, the style of cooking there has influenced me greatly. Food was presented in the dishes it was cooked in - very similar to modern-day Balti cooking - but the thing that struck me more than anything was the enormous amount of oil that was used. The curries were served up sometimes with an inch of oil or ghee floating on the surface. It was a fitness freak's nightmare - but everyone seemed to think that the more oil there was, the tastier the dish. You'll see in my recipe for Rogan Josh later in this book, that while it contains a lot of oil, the majority is strained off to make it healthier, and more attractive to British tastes.

The chef introduced me to a group of eight people eating in the restaurant. They immediately invited me to join them and share some of the food that I'd just seen cooking in the kitchen. This sociable way of eating is not out of the ordinary in that particular part of the world, and I was quickly made to feel like part of their group. Minutes later, several dishes appeared and were put in the middle of the table. The only place-setting for each person was a single plate. Within seconds, everyone had chapattis and were dipping them in the dishes - and they ate from them all. There were hands crossing all over the table, but still the friendly conversation continued, and there was a real sense of occasion. Having spent so much time in Britain, I found the huge amount of oil somewhat difficult to cope with but, as they say, "When in Karachi…". Although delicious, it *felt* unhealthy.

My brief visit to Pakistan was over. The next port of call was the area of Chittagong in my homeland of Bangladesh. One of the first things to hit you about the way they eat there, is that it's geared more towards rice. Whereas in Pakistan it was curries and chapattis, here pilau rice was served with almost every curry. Again, I was eager to get out of the towns and built up areas, so I immediately went exploring local villages. In one, I came across a small coffee shop and got talking to various people to find somewhere to stay. The "hotel" turned out to be somewhat less luxurious than the one I'd stayed at in Pakistan. I was taken to, basically, a shed where there were several beds - a sort of primitive dormitory. But, with the nearest Holiday Inn several hundred miles away, it was home for the night - ahead of a day exploring the mango plantations. After being woken by the intense sunlight, I chose a direction at random and headed off. I met a man who had lived in the area all his life and, when he heard about my search for the perfect curry, practically insisted that I go back to his mansion and have a meal with him. Of course, it's rude to say no. Later that day, I found myself being taken - on horseback - to a huge plantation house. It must have had at least thirty bedrooms, and hundreds of servants, most of whom had been working in the fields during the day.

There was a large karahi - or wok - in a communal area outside the house. Nearby, two whole goats, marinated in spices, were roasting on a spit above a wood fire. Sitting on a chair in the middle of this "kitchen" was an elderly man who told me his job was to cook for the family. Actually, that wasn't strictly true. He would direct the servants telling them to add one spoon of this, and another spoon of that, to this giant sizzling wok. This expert chef had it all planned out. It seemed to be as much about timing as it was about knowing how much spice to include. The cooking process started at 7pm and by precisely 11 o'clock it was ready. The dish itself was immense - and certainly trying to describe it here can't convey the sight of such a massive curry. A whole drum of oil was put into the wok, followed by at least a kilo of garlic and a slightly smaller amount of ginger - which they'd beaten in a giant mortar and pestle. Then the spices, which were measured by the spoonful - although "spade" is probably a more accurate description. The roasted goat was added, along with a large amount of salt, and allowed to simmer and cook right through. At 11pm, the family was summoned to join the servants and enjoy the feast in the courtyard. The curry was unbelievably good - especially so, as it had been cooked in such a mass-produced way for so many people. But again there was so much oil! I asked if I could drain some of it away - but they just laughed and said "that's why you're so thin!!". By my own standards I was far from thin but, looking around, I felt like the most athletic person there. My hosts were really big people, and I mean REALLY big. One man appeared to weigh more than 25 stone - but in this particular culture, where oil seems to be an essential part of the diet, that's not seen as unhealthy.

The following morning I was offered breakfast of plain roasted lamb. It was completely unseasoned - no spices had been used at all. The family were simply cutting slices of the meat and eating it with fresh roti, accompanied by a pint of tea. In England, curry is accompanied by a pint of beer - in Bangladesh, it's tea. Not unsurprisingly, with lots and lots of sugar.

Staying at the mansion was certainly not the healthiest eating experience I'd ever had, but it did teach me two things. Firstly, that mass-produced cooking can still have the most unbelievable texture and flavour if done correctly. And secondly, that I don't really like too much oil!

While in Bangladesh, as part of my quest, I had the privilege of another hillside cooking experience. I was strolling around the countryside during a particularly hot morning, with a chef friend of mine. A short way along one of the many hill tracks that make up the mountainous terrain, we bumped into a group of six or seven people walking along, just singing to themselves. Their daily task was to wander the countryside to ward off tigers. My friend and I told them what we were up to and asked if we could tag along. As with everywhere I visited on this trip, they were more than happy to accept our company, and we headed off into the hills.

After a few hours of warding off the tigers (they must have been good at it as we never saw a single one!), it was mealtime. They had brought with them some form of game - similar to a deer but slightly smaller - which they'd already killed. It had been skinned and was being carried around in a sack. A separate bag contained various other ingredients and assorted bits of cookware. They seemed more prepared than their counterparts in Nepal, and took out their "deer" and began dicing it with knives. As before, a large wok-like dish was used. But instead of resembling the traditional Balti, this was slightly deeper and a different shape. It was more like a flat cauldron.

Again, they'd chosen a spot where the spices grew naturally. They knew exactly what was growing where. Ginger and garlic were high on their list of ingredients, and they pulled large amounts out of the ground along with some incredibly strong tasting small onions - similar to shallots - but much stronger. It seemed obvious from this, that their strength and pungency would overpower the meat. Lots of oil, again, was used - reminding me of my coronary-inducing feast a few nights previously. Being the prepared group that they were, they had taken a large bottle of the oil with them. It wasn't the sort of oil we're used to in this country, it was more a palm oil or something similarly cheap. Rummaging in their sack, they produced some potatoes and a vegetable that I didn't recognise - but was similar to broccoli. They made the curry in a very traditional way - but with these really fresh and strong ingredients, it had a flavour that I've not been able to re-create since. It was also very spicy and even I had difficulty with its "stronger-than-vindaloo" taste. By the time the meal was ready to serve, there were fifteen of us all sitting round the fire, chatting and discussing the issues of the day. It all seems a far cry from the way many of us "pop out for a sandwich" at lunchtime and then rush back to the office.

After this rather large and somewhat over-spiced meal, I was invited to spend the afternoon with my newfound friends who gave me a guided tour of their "office" - several acres of rugged hillside where they pointed out many of their alternative cooking locations. There were substantial supplies of roots and onions, along with a plethora of spices and herbs growing wild. By nightfall the tables were about to be turned - "You're a chef", they said, "You wanted to see how we cooked. Let's see what YOU can do! It's your turn to cook for us".

So, the challenge had been set. I was handed a supply of spices, some meat, the wok and left to get on with it. Not surprisingly, I'd never cooked in these conditions before, and had always had the luxury of using pre-ground spices. They had no grinder, just a stone plate and a lump of wood similar to a rolling pin for crushing spices and onions.

I started off with the oil - but they repeatedly insisted that I wasn't using enough. No matter how much I tried to convince them that such huge amounts of oil are unhealthy, they simply wouldn't listen. Their unrelenting approach is that oil is good for you, and they want a lot of it floating on the top of the curry. They believe that the more you have, the more the body becomes "oily" and it stops you from becoming ill.

With my healthy living message going unheeded, I started cooking using the remaining half of the "deer" that they'd been carrying around with them all day. I was surprised to find out just how satisfying it was to cook using the most basic of techniques.

It's worth pointing out that hygiene seems to be largely ignored in this particular part of the world. I was beginning to wonder about eating this meat, which had hardly been kept in the freshest state. Still, we all survived, so it can't have been that hazardous. My customers today should be reassured that this lack of attention to hygiene is not one of the techniques I employ in my kitchens!

The dish I prepared was similar to the popular Dopiaza, which is a favourite among curry-lovers today. I wanted to make something slightly different to the meals they were used to, so, instead of using crushed shallots, I kept them whole. Despite their protestations that it wouldn't work, I decided to press on. In an attempt to be even more innovative, I used whole garlic cloves - again much to their disapproval. Growing nearby was a vegetable, similar in taste and texture to a cucumber, but it was small and round. I have no idea what it was called and have certainly never seen one in Britain, but it gave the dish a new dimension, which sadly doesn't work by putting normal cucumbers into curries here. The looks on their faces were getting ever more dismissive - and I began to wonder if they'd even TASTE this food, let alone LIKE it.

My fears were unfounded. In all my experience as a chef, I've never seen a reaction like it. They loved this curry, and were amazed that the combination of ingredients worked. These cucumber-like plants grow everywhere in this part of the world, but they'd never tried them in curries - only salads. So, with a rather smug air of satisfaction, I left them to enjoy the fruits of my labours, and headed back to my accommodation.

What they learned from me was minuscule compared with the experience that I'd gained from them. Their influence on me still lives on to this day, but I like to think that they still reminisce about the time when an English-trained chef turned up, eager to learn Balti cooking, and introduced them to a new dish.

Sadly, my travels around deepest Asia were over, and it was back to Britain to work in the restaurant. I'd been away for a total of six months, during which time I'd spent days in restaurant kitchens with professional chefs but, most importantly, I'd had the chance to see how real people cook real curries from real ingredients. It all seems a far cry from today's image of a busy restaurant on a Friday night at pub-closing-time, but those dishes which are appreciated by so many of my customers really do hail from my short but happy time on those remote mountain sides and hill tracks. It also makes it more of a pleasurable experience for me to cook curries - as each dish I prepare reminds me of those magical times learning the art of Balti cuisine.

When you try some of the Balti curries in this book, the first thing that you'll notice is that the preparation stage is rather time consuming. Worth it, but time consuming. However, there is one particular incident in my childhood which shows that long in-depth recipes aren't necessarily the way to make wonderful Asian food. Sometimes the simplest things are the best - as I hope you'll see from the "starters and accompaniments" section.

As a young child, I was sitting outside our large house in Bangladesh with my grandmother. I was part of a big family of about 35 people, and so a huge house was a necessity rather than a luxury! As is typical in households across the world, the nightly "what are we going to have for tea?" debate was well underway. My mother and grandmother were deep in conversation, and when it became apparent that they weren't going to reach a conclusion they turned to me and asked what I'd like. "Murghi Masala" was my instant reply. It's basically a chicken curry which we often used to eat when we had guests or on special occasions. "Murghi Masala it is then" was the reply, and one of the servants was duly despatched to get two dozen spring chickens. They're tiny birds, and very regularly used in cooking in that part of the world. The meat is marinated in a combination of aromatic spices, and each family has its own unique blend.

All the women in the house clubbed together to prepare the chicken, while another servant went to get all the necessary spices used in the marinade.

Marinating is a lengthy process - taking several hours - but, boys being boys, I was impatient, and wanted my chicken now. "But you have to let the meat marinate for several hours" came the reply, which only made me more determined! In the end, they relented and brought a small portable cooker and cooked the chicken right there for me, despite only having around half an hour of marinating time.

I've since eaten in many top restaurants across the globe - and tried some of the best food that the world has to offer. But, there was just something about that particular spiced chicken that I'll never forget. Never since have I eaten chicken like it. Maybe it was because I was young and naïve and was just beginning to explore the world of food but, since that day, Murghi Masala has been one of my favourite dishes. It also proves that you don't have to spend hours and hours preparing something for it to be as good as a dish you'd find in a top restaurant. It's still popular among my friends, family and customers, although many British people still tend to prefer the meat-in-sauce curries, rather than picking meat off the bone. But, my Murghi Masala usually changes their minds! Once you've mastered the basic Balti on page 25, have a go at the Chicken Tikka recipe in the "starters and accompaniments" section. It's a version of the Murghi Masala, which I remember from decades ago. Even served on it's own, it's a delightful dish.

My aim in the following chapters is to share with you the techniques I have learned on my travels. I use them everyday in preparing the hundreds of curries we serve at my "Kushi Balti House" in Birmingham's bustling Balti Triangle. I hope the last few pages have made you hungry and eager to get on with the fascinating business of cooking delicious curries to impress your friends and families. That's what this book is all about!

Notes

Chapter Two

Shopping for the ingredients

A quick flick through the recipes in this book may throw up ingredients that you've never heard of. Please don't let that put you off. Many spices are becoming more and more available, and going out and buying the ingredients can be as fascinating and rewarding as making the dishes themselves.

This chapter is designed to make shopping for the more exotic ingredients easy and, hopefully, stress-free.

Many of the ingredients in the recipes are widely available. Supermarkets are becoming more and more aware of the need to stock a wider range, and with the ethnic population of Great Britain becoming more and more diverse, the selection becomes increasingly interesting.

The main problem that you may encounter is getting hold of the spices. Many supermarkets will stock MOST of what you need, but you can bet that there'll be just a few essential ingredients that they've run out of - or just don't stock at all.

Before you even go to the supermarket for jars of spices and the like, it's well worth trying your local ethnic retailer. Depending on where you live, this may be just one small independent store, or a whole community of shops, mini-markets and small family businesses. Many large cities now have a bustling community made up of people from a variety of Asian cultures - and this is the best place to start. It's very rare for them not to stock something you need.

As an example, we'll use one of Britain's biggest and most thriving Asian communities - Birmingham. As with many other large cities, there are suburbs which are almost exclusively Asian and these are fascinating places to shop. The areas of Sparkhill, Small Heath and the famous "Balti triangle" are the best examples of this. There are rows upon rows of family-run shops selling everything from huge bags of spices and rice, to frozen fish and meat. They're also a great place to do your regular shopping - as you'll find the prices as competitive as any supermarket.

Huge selections of fresh produce, some unrecognisable to many English shoppers - plus essentials like chillies and peppers.

You'll also get a feel for the culture behind the dishes that you're cooking - as many shop owners will be more than happy to talk to you and advise you on what you're buying. These shops are incredibly friendly places and I can more-or-less guarantee that if you visit them again, you'll be treated like part of the family.

Many shops in such busy Asian communities will display selections of their produce out on the pavement - but inside, they're a maze with shelves full of aromatic spices, and ingredients from every corner of the world.

Some will have a fresh produce section, featuring fruit and vegetables - some of which you may not even recognise. If you're feeling a little experimental, have a chat to the shop assistants, who'll be more than happy to tell you what things are - and how best to eat them.

The spices you'll need for the recipes in this book are easily found in these shops. Bear in mind, though that they may be labelled differently from what you'd expect - and sometimes in different languages. If you're not sure, find someone to help or translate.

It's worth knowing a few of the most common translations. They are:

Dhaniya = Coriander
Jeera = Cumin
Haldi = Turmeric
Mehti = Fenugreek

The majority of the spices are available in small plastic bags (right), rather than the jars that you may be used to at the supermarket. You'll also find that they're significantly cheaper - which means that you can buy all the spices you need to get started for only a few pounds. (For up-to-date information on buying the spices you'll need in this book, please visit the book's internet site at **www.baltibook.co.uk**). These shops are also a

Hundreds of different spices - mainly sold in plastic bags.

great place to buy produce like garlic, ginger and onions. They sell so much of them that they're able to keep their prices really low. I regularly shop along the Coventry Road at Small Heath in Birmingham for fresh produce for my restaurant. This means it's guaranteed 100% fresh, of the best quality, and occasionally cheaper than bulk retailers.

Many restaurant owners also buy large quantities of rice from these shops, and you'll find dozens of different types. You're also able to buy it by the sack load.

Rice - in quantity!

Just to put things into perspective, a restaurant such as mine - which has a steady stream of visitors during the week but is packed out on Friday and Saturday nights - will get through five 25kg bags of onions a week. You won't need anywhere near that amount, but just spare a thought for restaurant staff who have to peel them and chop them up!

Normally stocked near the rice are the accompaniments - in particular popadoms. Everyone knows them as the large crisp-like starters you get in curry houses - but they start life as brittle discs, about the same size as a side plate, which expand rapidly when deep-fried. You can buy them ready made in supermarkets - but they're a great thing to try to cook yourself by buying them raw. Popadoms are made from finely ground flour - mixed with derivatives of shrimp - although many people can't taste any fishiness at all. Vegetarians should check the labels. They're available in different flavours, plain or spicy, and are delicious served with a cool yoghurt and mint dip (see the "accompaniments" section) or a selection of mango chutneys and lime pickle. Many restaurants make a stock of popadoms in advance, ready for the evening's business. One of the reasons for this is that, even though they only take seconds to make, they have to rest for about 15 minutes to cool down and crisp up before they're ready to eat. I make them daily so they're fresh but, if you're trying them at home, they can be stored overnight in an airtight container.

Cakes are a major feature of Asian stores - and you'll find a large selection ranging from cakes and biscuits to pastries and sweets. While touring the shops, you may notice that one of the most well-stocked cake products is something similar to a sponge cake but it's dry and crispy - rather like toast in consistency. This is usually labelled cake rusk, and looks like dry madeira cake cut into slices. It's well worth a try, and is normally served with tea of coffee.

One word of warning - don't expect it to be like typical English cake. Moist is certainly not the word! It's also enjoyed in Bangladesh with a drink of warm milk mixed with ground cashew nuts. That's worth trying as well - not least for the fact that it's believed in Asian countries to give you a long and healthy life - and to improve virility!

A selection of Asian speciality cakes. Well worth a try - but nothing like Victoria Sponge!

But it's not just about food: to cook the recipes in the following pages you'll need to buy some traditional Balti woks - or "karahi". Many shops will have them in different sizes and designs - and are essential for giving your guests that authentic Balti experience. Catering suppliers will also be able to get hold of them. Pickle trays, rice plates and other items of cookware are also readily available. If you can't find what you're looking for, just ask. If that shop doesn't stock it, they'll happily point you in the direction of someone who does. Some high street stores now sell them as part of gift-sets, and they can even be found in some supermarkets. Balti bowls can come in many shapes and sizes - and some of the thinner ones are only suitable for serving curries rather than cooking them. Make sure you have one which is right for your type of hob.

Because most of these shops are found in clusters in Asian communities, it's also worthwhile taking a stroll around the other ethnic stores nearby.

A colourful display of fresh fruit outside a typical shop on Birmingham's bustling Stratford Road.

Many areas (particularly in big cities like Birmingham and London) will be a mix of shops, markets and companies catering for the Asian community, as well as banks and places of worship. You'll more than likely find shops specialising in fabrics from the subcontinent and also a proliferation of sweet shops. These are fascinating places - and the owner or shopkeeper will be happy to be your guide.

This type of shop is a great place to pop into on the day of your curry-dinner-party to pick up some desserts. They will not only be different to those your guests are used to, but also make for a very attractive centrepiece when it comes to serving

the coffee at the end. As you'll see from the photograph (right), we're talking about a cross between a cake and a sweet here. In many of the bigger shops you'll find them laid out more like Belgian chocolates in a continental *chocolaterie*. Pick 'n' mix, however, IS the order of the day.

Be warned though: these Asian sweets can be rather too sweet for the British palate but, in moderation or enjoyed with a cup of tea, they can be a fascinating treat. Many of the "sweet centres" will offer a wide variety - and will sell them either individually or by the box. If you're new to this type of food, it's worth explaining this so the shopkeeper can advise you on what may be best to try first. You'll no doubt go back again and again - but it's advisable to experiment a little before buying for your dinner party as you'll probably be able to predict what your guests will enjoy most.

Sweet treats on display. But ask before you buy! Many shop owners will know what are best to tempt the British palate.

Without wishing to deter you, Asian sweets like these are not the healthiest things in the world. DIABETICS SHOULD BE AWARE. Many are made with large quantities of sugar and clarified butter or ghee. Having said that, the intense flavours will probably stop you eating more than just a few at a time.

I'd love to be able to talk more about these delicacies, as they are unfortunately overlooked when it comes to "going out for a curry" - but that would probably be an entire book in itself. The reason they're not widely recognised is simply that deserts have never been a big part of the restaurant curry scene. Most chefs operate on limited resources, and put all their time and energy into making their curry dishes and creating new ways to present them. If we're honest though, most customers tend not to have room for dessert after a meal - and those who do, normally want something comparatively simple, like an ice cream or kulfi (a yoghurt-based frozen dessert).

To conclude, a brief note about "Halal meat" - which is a term you'll see a lot in many of these shopping communities. Several cultures put a great emphasis on the concept of "Halal" - which describes meat that's been slaughtered in accordance with a particular religion. It may be a gruesome thing to think about but people of certain religions will only eat meat which has been killed by a certified person who performs the act in a particular way. Many years ago, I used to do this for a living. The slaughter would be carried out under strict conditions and the meat would then be stamped as being "genuine Halal" and shipped out to butchers as being killed in the name of a spiritual sacrifice.

"Halal" meat has simply a spiritual significance, and is not necessarily required for the recipes in this book.

Remember also that this book has its own website - **www.baltibook.co.uk** - where you can find up-to-date information on ways to locate the spices you'll need for the recipes. It also contains a list of recommended suppliers.

Chapter Three

The three basic components

 Please read this page. It's one of the most important in the book when it comes to cooking curries. Don't skip ahead!!

When you order a Balti curry in a restaurant, it can be ready in as little as five minutes. This is because it's a mixture of several pre-cooked components, and combinations of spices made earlier in the day. These are expertly blended together on the night, and freshly cooked to give the completed dish, served sizzling at your table. Most restaurants will prepare huge quantities of these sauces, pre-cooked meats and spices ready for a busy night's trade.

This chapter will show you how to make the three basic components and will then guide you through the simple stages of cooking Balti curries, starting with the most popular - a Basic Balti. This can be Balti Chicken, Balti Lamb, Balti Vegetable, or Balti Prawn.

It's not a quick process. It will take a few hours to prepare the individual components, but only minutes when you come to serve the dish to your guests. I recommend that you take a few moments to read through this entire chapter first, to get a feel for the whole process, so it will all make more sense when you start cooking.

After the Basic Balti recipe is a brief explanation in chapter five of how to make it hotter. This includes MADRAS, VINDALOO and PHALL which require only minor modifications.

Following that, we'll move on to more elaborate Balti dishes. The procedure is very similar for each one. In fact, once you've made the basic Balti, it's really a question of adding things to it, or simply adapting the recipe. This section includes the relatively simple BHUNA, DOPIAZA, and PATHIA. After that, the recipes get a little more advanced, with a ROGAN JOSH - which is quite an interesting dish to prepare, as it involves a special garnish. Then, the chapter ends with Balti DHANSAK, which includes a recipe for a plain DHAL. The dhal is a delicious accompaniment on its own.

The chart on the next page shows how it all works.

As previously mentioned, don't expect perfection the first time you try. I've tried to make the recipes here as simple to follow as possible, so you learn along the way. But, take your time, follow the recipes, and most importantly, have fun! Please don't be put off by the long lists of ingredients - you'll soon see that it's a very easy and rewarding process.

Many of the recipes use standard teaspoon and tablespoon measures for spices. It's a good idea to buy a set of measuring spoons containing a tablespoon, teaspoon, half teaspoon and quarter of a teaspoon. (One tablespoon is 15ml and a teaspoon is 5ml.)

Some of the recipes call for a ladle to be used. In the restaurant, we use a 125ml ladle which is probably slightly larger than many domestic ones. The amount you need depends really on individual taste, but use 125ml as a guideline.

This book also has its own website at **www.baltibook.co.uk** containing up-to-the-minute troubleshooting advice for the recipes, and lists recommended suppliers. It's worth checking the website before starting cooking, for any additional hints and tips on the dish you're making.

Combining the ingredients

Our first dish is the plain and simple Balti.

Before cooking, you'll need to decide what sort of base "meat" you want it to be. For the purposes of this book, this can be chicken, lamb, vegetable or prawn. Although described as "plain and simple" this is a wonderfully flavoursome dish, and one of the most popular restaurant curries, best served with freshly cooked, fluffy pilau rice.

The basic Balti is made up of three essential components, which are shown on the left of the diagram below. These all need to be prepared in advance - preferably on the day of your Balti dinner party. Once this has been done, it only takes a few minutes to make the basic Balti itself.

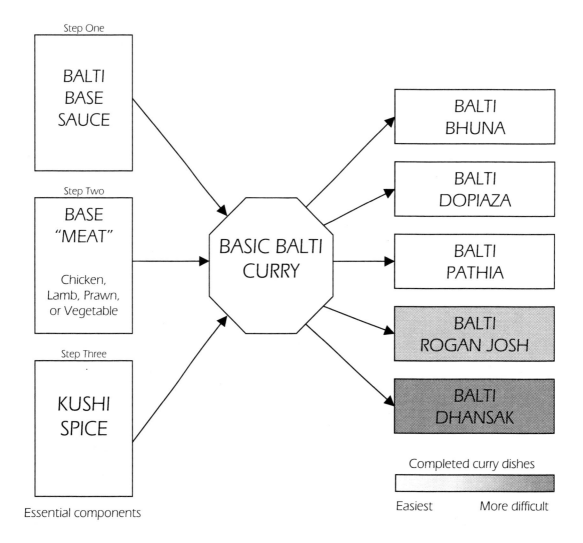

Once you've made the basic Balti curry (in the middle of the diagram), a few adaptations will turn it into any of the dishes on the right. They get slightly harder as they go down, but it never really gets TOO difficult.

The three essential components are:

- BALTI BASE SAUCE. This is a spiced onion gravy, which restaurants make in huge quantities, and provides the bulk of the sauce you get in a Balti curry. (Preparation: just over 1 hour).

- BASE "MEAT". Whether you choose chicken, lamb or vegetable, it's cooked in a blend of spices, so it's ready to be made into a Balti curry. (Preparation: up to 1 hour). Prawn doesn't require any advance preparation, as it's bought pre-cooked. The procedure to follow when making the final dish, though, varies slightly.

- KUSHI SPICE. This is a special combination of spices, which will be used throughout this book. It shouldn't be confused with "garam masala" or supermarket-bought "mixed spice". We'll call it "Kushi" spice, after my restaurant, to distinguish it from any other type of spice mixture. (Preparation: a few minutes).

Once these are prepared, you have everything you need to make a Balti curry in just a few minutes.

 It's also recommended that you cook and serve your completed dishes in a Balti bowl (or "karahi"). These are now quite widely available. See chapter two for hints on where to find them.

Ingredients for dishes in this chapter

The quantities shown are for roughly 4-5 portions of base "meat". The quantity of base sauce is for approximately 10 portions.

BALTI BASE SAUCE (page 15)

3 cloves
2 cinnamon sticks (3-4 inches long)
3-4 pieces mace
3-4 green cardamom pods
2 star anise
Pinch fenugreek seed
3 bay leaves, dried
1 kg onion, coarsely chopped
1½ tbsp salt
½ green pepper
½ red pepper
125g fresh carrot, chopped
25g fresh coriander leaf
10-15g fresh garlic (about 3-4 cloves)
10-15g peeled ginger (similar quantity to garlic)
¾ tsp chilli powder
1¼ tsp coriander powder
½ tsp cumin powder
½ tsp turmeric powder
1 tsp curry powder
1¼ tsp dried fenugreek leaves, chopped
¾ tsp garam masala powder
200g tin of chopped tomato
4 tbsp (60ml) vegetable oil

BASE CHICKEN (page 18)

1 kg chicken fillets, cubed
15-20g fresh garlic (about 4-5 cloves)
20g fresh ginger (similar quantity to garlic)
¼ tsp chilli powder
¾ tsp turmeric powder
¼ tsp cumin powder
½ tsp coriander powder
½ tsp curry powder
¼ tsp garam masala
½ tsp salt
6 tbsp (90ml) vegetable oil
200g tin chopped tomato

BASE LAMB (page 20)

1 kg lamb - leg is best
6 tbsp (90ml) vegetable oil
15-20g fresh garlic (about 4-5 cloves)
20g fresh ginger (similar quantity to garlic)
1½ tsp salt
1½ tsp sugar
200g tin chopped tomato
½ tsp chilli powder
1½ tsp turmeric powder
½ tsp cumin powder
¾ tsp coriander powder
¾ tsp curry powder
¼ tsp garam masala powder

BASE VEGETABLE (page 21)

1 kg mixed vegetables
(we recommend 125g each of potato, carrot, peas, green beans, mushrooms, cauliflower, broccoli and sweetcorn)

2 medium onions, chopped
8-9 garlic cloves
2¼ tsp chilli powder
1½ tsp turmeric powder
½ tsp cumin powder
1¼ tsp coriander powder
1 tsp curry powder
4-5 bay leaves
2½ cinnamon sticks (3-4 inches long)
5 green cardamom pods
2 black cardamom pods
4 cloves
3 star anise
5 tbsp vegetable oil
1 tbsp salt

BASE PRAWN (page 22)

For the dishes in this book, use pre-cooked prawns, as bought from the supermarket. No pre-preparation is required. We recommend 300g fresh cooked prawns per Balti dish.

"KUSHI" SPICE (page 23)

½ tsp chilli powder
3 tsp turmeric powder
1 tsp cumin powder
2½ tsp coriander powder
2 tsp curry powder
1½ tsp garam masala powder
1 tsp garlic powder
½ tsp ginger powder
2 tsp dried fenugreek leaf, chopped

For help in finding the spices you'll need for these recipes, please see chapter two - or the book's website:
www.baltibook.co.uk

Balti Base Sauce

This recipe will make about 10 portions. It'll be used in future chapters, from Balti chicken, to Dhansak, to Rogan Josh and so on.

Start with a clean piece of cooking net and a very large saucepan. (A pressure-cooker size should do. It may not seem big enough at the start, but the onions soon sweat down and decrease in size.)

Into the net, place:

- 3 cloves
- 2 cinnamon sticks (each 3-4 inches long)
- 3-4 pieces of mace
- 3-4 green cardamom pods
- 2 star anise
- Pinch of fenugreek seed
- 3 bay leaves, dried

Then tie a knot - making it similar to a large tea-bag.   Drop this into the saucepan, along with:

- 1 kg onion, roughly chopped
- 1½ tbsp salt
- 450ml (¾ pint) cold water
- ½ green and ½ red pepper, chopped
- 125g fresh carrot, roughly chopped
- 25g fresh coriander leaves

Stir well.

Put onto a high heat, and bring to the boil. Cover and simmer for 45 minutes, stirring frequently.

While that's simmering, make another mixture to add to it. Take:

- 10-15g peeled fresh garlic (about 3-4 cloves)
- 10-15g peeled fresh ginger (similar to the amount of garlic)

Using a blender, make into a paste with a small amount of water. Set aside.

Then, in a separate bowl, mix:

- ¾ tsp chilli powder
- 1¼ tsp coriander powder
- ½ tsp cumin powder
- 1½ tsp turmeric powder
- 1 tsp curry powder
- 1¼ tsp dried fenugreek leaf, finely chopped
- ¾ tsp garam masala powder

Open a 200g can of chopped tomato and set aside.

◀ Into a separate, good-sized saucepan (we've used a Balti bowl in the pictures), add 4 tbsp (60 ml) of vegetable oil. Heat the oil then add the garlic and ginger paste mixture. Stir until it becomes golden brown.

Take off the heat, and add the mixture of spices. It's important to remove it from the heat, as spices burn easily, and should be treated with care.

Stir well, and return to a very low heat. You'll notice the wonderful instant aroma of spices.

Add the can of chopped tomato, and bring the mixture to the boil, stirring constantly. ▶

◀ Add 600ml (1 pint) of hot water into the mixture, and bring back to the boil, stirring constantly. Despite the fact that there's now liquid in this mixture, the spices can still burn on the base of the pan.

Once it has boiled for about a minute, take it off the heat.

Go back to the large pan of onion mixture. Once it's boiled for the necessary 45 minutes, remove the net containing the whole spices, and throw it away.

Pour the spicy tomato mixture into the onion pan, stir well, and boil for around five minutes. ▶

◀ Leave to cool and then reduce to a smooth gravy using a blender.

The "base sauce" is now complete, and you're now well on the way to making a restaurant-style Balti.

This sauce can be stored in the fridge until you're ready to use it. Freezing it IS possible - but this can impair the flavour.

The next step is to make pre-cooked base 'meat'.

Base "Meat"

Now, you'll need to decide what sort of "meat" you want in your first curry.

I use inverted commas around the word meat because, as previously mentioned, this can be a mixture of vegetables instead.

For the purposes of this book, there are four types of base "meat".

Chicken - This is probably the most popular meat chosen in restaurants. It's also slightly easier than lamb to prepare, as it doesn't need the same amount of care and attention to keep it tender.

Lamb - Undeniably a restaurant favourite, but needs to be cooked properly, so that it's not too tough. It's always good to get this from your butcher, to make sure it's lean, and of the highest quality. Somehow diced "casserole-type" lamb from the supermarket just doesn't seem to work.

Vegetable - Of course, curries don't have to contain meat. Vegetarians can rest assured that the other two components (base sauce and Kushi Spice) are perfectly suitable for their diet, and none of the dishes contains any meat stock.

Prawn - For the purposes of this book, we'll use pre-cooked prawns - easily available from supermarkets.

For base chicken, turn to page 18

For base lamb, go to page 20

For base vegetable, page 21

For base prawn, see page 22

After making the base "meat", you'll then be directed to page 23, where you'll make the final component, Kushi Spice.

Pre-cooked chicken (base)

This will make around 4-5 portions, which - like the base sauce - will be used in future dishes.

This recipe involves a certain amount of preparation before the cooking actually begins. It's important to have everything to hand. Base chicken takes slightly less time than to cook than its lamb equivalent, and is no more difficult than making an average stir-fry. Many people find dealing with chicken much easier than lamb, so this recipe is a good starting point. You'll need a large flat saucepan capable of holding the amount of chicken in the recipe - although a wok works just as well.

1 kg of chicken breast fillet, cut into 1 inch cubes

15-20g (about 4-5 cloves) garlic
20g fresh peeled ginger (similar to the amount of garlic)

¼ tsp chilli powder
¾ tsp turmeric powder
¼ tsp cumin powder
½ tsp coriander powder
½ tsp curry powder
¼ tsp garam masala powder
½ tsp salt

6 tbsp (90ml) vegetable oil
A 200g tin of chopped tomato

Take the chicken breast fillets and cut into one inch cubes, and set aside.

Place the garlic and ginger into a blender, and reduce to a paste using around 2 tbsp of cold water to help make it smooth.

Set this aside.

 If you haven't got a blender which will work with such small quantities of ingredients, you can buy jars containing garlic paste or puréed ginger in supermarkets, which are just as effective. Add them in the proportions shown. Alternatively, you can use shredded garlic for extra "boost".

Then into a separate bowl place all the powdered spices - along with the salt.

Give this a very thorough mix to make sure they're all combined.

Set aside.

◀ Pour the vegetable oil into a large saucepan or wok, and place onto a high heat.

Add the garlic and ginger, and fry until it's golden brown, stirring regularly. It may spit to start with.

Take it off the heat, and add the spice mixture.

Again, put it back on a LOW heat, and stir constantly for a few seconds, so the spices don't burn. ▶

◀ Add the tomatoes, and bring to the boil, while stirring.

Add the diced chicken, and mix well. ▶

◀ Simmer for five minutes, stirring regularly.

Then, cover and simmer for a further ten minutes, stirring occasionally.

Take off the heat.

The base chicken is now ready, and once cooled, can be refrigerated. It can be eaten on its own as a very mild dish (although it's not a complete curry) and is particularly popular with children.

The third and final step is to make "Kushi Spice". Please go to page 23.

Pre-cooked lamb (base)

This will make around 4-5 portions, which - like the base sauce - will be used in future dishes.

1kg of lamb, leg is best - cut into 1 inch cubes
200g tin of chopped (or plum) tomato
6 tbsp (90ml) vegetable oil

15-20g (about 4-5 cloves) garlic
20g fresh peeled ginger (similar to the amount of garlic)

½ tsp chilli powder
1½ tsp turmeric powder
½ tsp cumin powder
¾ tsp coriander powder
¾ tsp curry powder
¼ tsp garam masala

1½ tsp salt
1½ tsp sugar

Using a blender, purée the garlic and ginger with 2 tbsp of water. Add this to the lamb, ▶ and mix well with your hands, as if you're "massaging" it into the meat.

Add the salt, sugar, and then the vegetable oil. Continue this "massaging" process to really tenderise the lamb. Add 100ml cold water. Stir well.

Put the mixture into a large saucepan, cover and simmer for 15-20 minutes, stirring regularly. ▶

Add the spices and tomato, and mix well. Keep stirring, so the spices don't burn. Once it's thoroughly mixed, boil for five minutes - uncovered, stirring constantly.

Reduce the heat and simmer for a further five, stirring occasionally.

The base lamb is now ready ▶ and once cooled, can be refrigerated. It can be eaten on its own as a very mild dish (although it's not a complete curry) and is particularly popular with children.

The third and final step is to make "Kushi Spice". Please go to page 23.

Pre-cooked mixed vegetables (base)

This flexible combination will make around 4-5 portions, which - like the base sauce - will be used in future dishes.

4-5 bay leaves
2½ cinnamon sticks (each 3-4 inches long)
5 green cardamom pods
2 black cardamom pods
4 cloves
3 star anise

1 kg mixed vegetables (to suit your taste, but see our recommendation below)

2 medium onions, finely chopped
8-9 garlic cloves, peeled

2¼ tsp chilli powder
1½ tsp turmeric powder
½ tsp cumin powder
1¼ tsp coriander powder
1 tsp curry powder

5 tbsp vegetable oil
1 tbsp salt

Place the whole spices (bay leaves, cinnamon, cardamom pods, cloves and star anise) into a clean piece of cooking net, and - as with the base sauce recipe - tie with a knot.

Drop the net into a saucepan containing 900ml (1½ pints) of water, and boil for about 20 minutes - or however long it takes to reduce to approximately half the original volume. Take the net out, and throw it away. Keep the spicy water to one side, as it'll be used later in the recipe.

While that's boiling, prepare the vegetables. This can be varied to suit your taste but the following is a typical restaurant combination:

125g potato - diced into 1cm pieces
125g carrot - cut into ½ cm slices
125g peas
125g green beans - cut into 1 cm lengths
125g mushrooms - cut into quarters
125g cauliflower - broken into pieces approximately 1½ cm in size
125g broccoli - broken into pieces approximately 1½ cm in size
125g sweetcorn (if using tinned, drain the water, and rinse thoroughly)

Prepare these individually, and put to one side.

Next, take the garlic and chop very finely or reduce to a paste in a blender. (This amount of garlic is necessary, because of the large amount of vegetables that we're using. It adds much needed flavour.) Again, put this to one side.

Place the powdered spices (chilli, turmeric, cumin, coriander and curry powder) into a bowl, mix well and set aside.

Pour the vegetable oil into a separate saucepan which is big enough to take all the vegetables. In fact, the bigger the better.

Place on a moderate heat. Add the garlic, and fry until golden brown.

Then add the onion until it too becomes golden brown, before adding 1 tbsp of salt. Mix well.

Reduce to a very low heat, and add the mixture of spices, stirring constantly to prevent it from burning.

Add about half of the spiced water mixture to the pan, and continue stirring.

On a low heat, and stirring constantly, add the carrot, and boil for three minutes. Then add the potato, leaving it to boil for another three minutes. Now add all the other vegetables - except the broccoli and sweetcorn. Leave them for about two or three minutes, before finally adding them, along with the rest of the spicy water. Let it cook gently until it's tender and most of the liquid has evaporated. (This should take about 10 minutes.)

See page 26 for a photograph of what base mixed vegetables will look like, to help you achieve the best results.

The mixed vegetable base is now ready and, once cooled, can be refrigerated. The third and final step is to make "Kushi Spice". Please go to page 23.

Pre-cooked prawn (base)

The base chicken, lamb and vegetables all need pre-cooking, so they're ready when you come to prepare your finished dish. Prawns are slightly different, as the recipes in this book (chapters 4 and 5) contain prawns which are bought pre-cooked. This makes it easier, as you don't have to spend the time cooking them to form your base.

The difference is that the other base "meats" are quite heavily spiced, which is taken into account when you make the completed dishes. If you're using prawn, you'll need to use more spice in the finished Balti, to make up for the fact they've not been seasoned in the same way the chicken, lamb or vegetables have during their preparation.

This is easy to do. When you get to the recipes themselves, you'll notice that each specifies a quantity of Kushi Spice. In brackets after this is the amount of Kushi Spice you'll need if you're using prawns. It's about double the normal quantity, but does vary slightly. It's as simple as that.

When the recipes for an individual dish refer to using a ladle full of base "meat", simply add around 300g of fresh cooked prawns. As bought from any supermarket.

The advantage of using prawns is that you save a lot of time and effort making the pre-cooked base, but I'd strongly recommend having a go at the chicken, lamb or vegetable bases first. This way, you'll get a much more thorough grounding in some of the cookery techniques which we'll use in other recipes in this book. It's also a useful confidence building exercise! The third and final step is now to make the "Kushi Spice". Please go to page 23.

Kushi Spice

Every restaurant has its own combination of mixed spice to give its dishes a unique flavour.

Most chefs keep this a closely guarded secret, as it defines the taste of a curry from their restaurant, and separates it from their competitors.

This recipe is my own personal version, which I've been using in restaurants for most of my career as a professional chef and, I believe, gives the best results.

To save confusion with other spice mixtures used throughout this book, we'll call it "Kushi" Spice - the same name as my restaurant.

½ tsp chilli powder
3 tsp turmeric powder
1 tsp cumin powder
2½ tsp coriander powder
2 tsp curry powder
1½ tsp garam masala powder
1 tsp garlic powder
½ tsp ginger powder
2 tsp dried fenugreek leaf, finely chopped

Place all the spices into a bowl and mix thoroughly. It's important to combine the ingredients completely, as we'll be using Kushi Spice in every curry in this book. Store it in a jar, or other airtight container, to keep it fresh and aromatic.

The three main components of the basic Balti dish are now ready. You can now move onto preparing the curry, which you only need to start cooking about ten minutes before you want to serve it.

 You may be concerned that individual ingredients don't smell or taste like a Balti curry. Don't worry! It's the way they're combined that transforms them into a restaurant-style dish. The next chapter shows you exactly how to do this.

The vast array of spices used in a typical restaurant.

Notes

Chapter Four

Making a basic Balti curry

ⓘ **If you've arrived here without making the three basic components of a Balti curry, you'll need to go back to page 11.**

This is the easy bit. A nice short chapter! It's the stage where the three basic components are transformed into a meal that you'd expect to get from a restaurant. The recipe is per portion, and uses one Balti bowl or karahi. If you really can't get hold of one, use a frying pan, and transfer onto a plate afterwards. Make sure the base sauce, base "meat" (chicken, lamb, vegetable or pre-cooked prawns) and Kushi Spice are easily to hand. For the purposes of the photographs in this recipe, chicken is the base meat - but, because whatever you use is pre-cooked anyway, the process is the same.

For an individual portion of Balti chicken, lamb, vegetable or prawn:

**1 garlic clove, finely chopped
¼ medium onion, finely chopped
2 tbsp vegetable oil
½ tomato, chopped**

Take a Balti bowl, and add the vegetable oil. Over a high heat, fry the garlic, until light brown. ▶

Add the onion, and fry for a minute or so, until golden brown.

Remove from the heat, and stir in 1½ tsp of "Kushi Spice" (3 tsp if you're using prawns as a base meat). Return to a low heat, stirring constantly to prevent burning.

Add a ladle-full of the pre-cooked 'meat' (chicken, lamb, vegetables or 300 grams of fresh cooked prawns) ▲ Simmer for about a minute.

Add a ladle of the base sauce (in the restaurant, the ladle size we use is 125ml), and bring to the boil, stirring constantly. ▶

Add the tomato, simmer for two minutes, garnish with fresh coriander leaves and **serve!**

Reference page

This page contains photographs to illustrate recipes in other parts of the book.

Pre-cooked mixed vegetables (base)

◄ This shows a smaller quantity than you'll get by following the recipe, to demonstrate in better detail, what sort of consistency you're aiming for.

Rogan Josh

Step one starts with the frying of the onions ◄ to make a basic curry ►

Step two cooks an oil-based mixture ◄ which is then used to garnish the completed dish ►

Adding pineapple and dhal ▼

Dhansak
...then, the base meat ▼

...and finally, base sauce ▼

Chapter Five

Elaborating on the basic Balti

Congratulations! You've now made your first curry dish - and hopefully, it was as good as you'd get in a restaurant.

This chapter contains recipes for some more "exotic" dishes. These are restaurant favourites and are variations on the theme of the basic Balti. Having made the basic dish, you should now *understand* the concept of making Baltis and the next few pages will be simple to follow. A few subtle changes can transform a curry into something a bit more special.

Madras, Vindaloo, Phall - page 28
changing the strength of a basic Balti curry

Tikka Balti Dishes - page 28
using marinated chicken or lamb instead of base meat

Bhuna - page 29
a Balti dish rich in tomato

Dopiaza - page 30
containing a generous quantity of onion

Pathia - page 31
hot and sour - and very popular!

Rogan Josh - page 32
a very rich dish, with a special garnish

Dhansak - page 33
the addition of lentils and pineapple makes this a fruity, hot dish

As you may recall from the flowchart on page 12, these dishes vary in difficulty.

Bhuna, Dopiaza and Pathia are relatively easy, while Rogan Josh and Dhansak involve slightly more preparation. For Rogan Josh, you effectively make two dishes, and use one to garnish the other. Dhansak requires you to make a plain and simple dhal - a lentil dish, which forms part of the completed curry.

 Make sure you still have enough base sauce, base meat and Kushi Spice to cook these dishes.

Start with the curry you'd probably choose in a restaurant and then try some of the others. You never know - your own home cookery could influence what you order the next time you go out for a meal in a Balti house.

Not hot enough for you? Changing the strength of the Basic Balti

With only a minor alteration you can make your Balti dish into a hotter curry - a Balti Madras.

Make the Balti by following the same procedure as before, but add one teaspoon of chilli powder at the same time as the 1½ teaspoons of Kushi Spice.

Always use 1½ teaspoons of Kushi Spice, but obviously, the more chilli powder, the hotter it gets.

There's nothing worse than a curry that's too hot to eat so start by using ½ teaspoon of chilli powder, and experiment from there.

One teaspoon of chilli powder turns it into a **Madras**.

Two teaspoons of chilli powder makes it a **Vindaloo**.

Three or more teaspoons of chilli powder creates a **Phall -** a very hot curry.

 Please try a Vindaloo before braving the fieriness of Phall. If you don't regret it at the time, you may do the following morning!

Normally the Phall is reserved only for those occasions when someone tries to show off by eating the hottest curry on the menu. I really don't recommend it.

Chicken / Lamb Tikka Balti dishes

Instead of the pre-cooked chicken or lamb, you can add an extra dimension to your Balti dishes by using chicken or lamb tikka - normally served as a starter - which is versatile enough to be used in Balti curry dishes.

Simply cook the tikka recipe on page 52, and add a portion to your dish in place of the ladle of base meat.

This is possible with the plain Balti, and any of the dishes in this chapter - for example to turn a Balti Lamb Pathia into a Balti Lamb Tikka Pathia.

Bhuna

Bhuna is a very popular medium strength dish. It has quite a simple flavour - and the generous use of tomatoes makes it a big hit in restaurants. It's fairly dry, but has a good mixture of spices and onion. I tend to recommend this to someone who's a "semi-beginner" to curries. A very mild Korma (see page 41) is best for those who've never experienced Balti before - but is too mild and creamy for some. In that case I recommend Bhuna, which is more of a traditional dish in appearance and taste, and one I find myself making many of in the restaurant.

Per portion:

2 tbsp vegetable oil
2 garlic cloves, finely chopped
1 medium onion, finely chopped
2 tsp Kushi Spice (see page 23) (use 3½ tsp Kushi Spice, if you're using prawns as a base meat)
Pinch of salt
A ladle of base "meat" (see page 17)
2 tomatoes, chopped
A ladle of base sauce (see page 15)
Fresh coriander leaves to garnish

Put the Balti bowl on a gentle heat.

Add the vegetable oil.

Add the garlic and onion and fry until golden brown. Remove from the heat.

Add the Kushi Spice, and a pinch of salt and stir quickly.

Then add some of the base 'meat' - the same amount as in the basic Balti.

Return to the heat, and add the tomatoes, stirring once again.

After a few minutes, add a ladle of the base sauce, and cook until it starts to boil.

Simmer for around five minutes, and the water content will evaporate. It should be quite a dry dish - unlike those we've made before. The sauce will become thicker and drier, the longer you heat the dish.

Garnish with fresh coriander leaves, and serve.

Dopiaza

This medium-hot restaurant favourite contains large pieces of chopped onion and has a full flavour. The preparation isn't really that different to a basic Balti but the addition of chunky - rather than finely chopped - onion transforms it into a completely individual dish.

Per portion:

2 tbsp vegetable oil
2 garlic cloves, finely chopped
½ tsp crushed ginger
1 large onion, chopped into ½ inch cubes
2 tsp Kushi Spice (see page 23) (use 4 tsp Kushi Spice, if you're using prawns as a base meat)
Pinch of salt
½ tsp chilli powder
Pinch of sugar
A ladle of base "meat" (see page 17)
A ladle of base sauce (see page 15)
Fresh coriander leaves to garnish

Place the Balti bowl on a moderate heat, and add the vegetable oil.

Add the garlic and ginger and fry until golden brown.

Add the onion and stir until it softens and begins to turn golden brown.

Add the Kushi Spice, and remove from the heat.

Then add the salt, chilli powder and sugar.

Return to a low heat, stirring constantly. Add the base 'meat' (the same amount as in the basic Balti) and turn up the heat.

Add a ladle of base sauce, and bring to the boil.

Simmer for 2-3 minutes and garnish with fresh coriander leaves.

Simmer for a further minute - and serve.

Pathia

Pathia is a hot and sour dish. Its taste is difficult to describe but, if you've never had it before, it's well worth making. Again, it's a simple dish, but the addition of fresh lemon juice gives it an edge you don't find with other Baltis. Not really a dish for someone new to Asian cuisine, but a joy for curry-holics.

Per portion:

2 tbsp vegetable oil
2 garlic cloves, finely chopped
1 medium onion, finely chopped
1 ½ tsp Kushi Spice (see page 23) (use 3 tsp Kushi Spice, if you're using prawns as a base meat)
¾ tsp chilli powder
2 tsp sugar
Juice of half a lemon
1 tomato, diced
A ladle of base "meat" (see page 17)
A ladle of base sauce (see page 15)
Fresh coriander leaves to garnish

Gently heat the vegetable oil in the Balti bowl.

Add the garlic and onion, and stir until it starts to turn golden brown. (If it goes completely brown, it won't give the right flavour.)

Remove from the heat, and immediately add the Kushi Spice and chilli powder, stirring constantly.

Add the sugar, lemon juice and tomato. Stir.

Return to a low heat and add a portion of the base 'meat' - the same amount as in the basic Balti.

Next, add one full ladle of base sauce, and bring to the boil.

Simmer for 2 minutes.

Garnish with fresh coriander leaves, and serve.

Rogan Josh

Rogan Josh is an elaborate dish to prepare, because it's slightly different to those we've done before. It's essentially a curry, garnished with a... curry!

Per portion:

STEP ONE
1 ½ tbsp of vegetable oil
1 garlic clove, chopped
½ medium sized onion, finely chopped
2 tsp of Kushi Spice (see page 23) (use 2½ tsp Kushi Spice, if you're using prawns as a base meat)
½ fresh tomato, chopped
A ladle of base "meat" (see page 17)
A ladle of base sauce (see page 15)
Fresh coriander leaves to garnish

STEP TWO
2 tsp vegetable oil
2 garlic cloves, crushed
½ onion, very finely chopped
1 teaspoon Kushi Spice (see page 23) (this quantity is unchanged if using prawns)
1 whole tomato, chopped

Step one makes a basic curry, which will then be garnished with the dish we make in step two.

STEP ONE Put the Balti bowl on the heat, add the vegetable oil. When it's fairly hot, add the garlic, and stir until slightly brown. Then, add the onion, and stir until it too becomes slightly brown. Take off the heat, add the Kushi Spice and chopped tomato, then heat gently for 30 seconds, stirring constantly.

Then add the base 'meat' followed by the base sauce. Stir constantly, and cook for about 2 minutes. Then let it simmer, on a low heat while you continue with step two.

STEP TWO Take a separate saucepan or Balti bowl. Add the vegetable oil, and bring to a moderate heat. Add the garlic until it browns, then add the onion until it too is golden brown. Remove from the heat, add the "Kushi Spice" and tomato, then cook for one minute until the tomato becomes soft and begins to fall apart.

Finally, pour the mixture from step two onto the curry you made in step one, to complete the whole dish. Don't mix them up, just sprinkle with fresh coriander leaves, and serve up the sizzling Balti immediately.

 Because of the way it's made, some people tend to find Rogan Josh a bit oily, but if you hold the dish at an angle you can spoon off some of the oil which floats to the surface - making it healthier and less greasy. Normally in the restaurant, I tend to remove as much of the oil as possible, but people have different tastes, so choose the amount that's right for you.

 See page 26 for photographs of the various stages of cooking Rogan Josh.

Dhansak

Like Rogan Josh, this is a combination of two dishes: Dhal, and a curry base.

You need a portion of dhal (see next page for the recipe), as well as the usual base sauce, base 'meat' and Kushi Spice.

The lentils add a very pleasant texture to curries and take away some of the bland-ness which people often find with plain Balti dishes.

Dhansak also includes a new element: pineapple. Many people instinctively think of citrus fruits being used in Chinese cookery - but they have a special place in Balti cuisine also, adding a different dimension to the taste.

Per portion:

1 tbsp vegetable oil
3 garlic cloves, crushed
1 medium onion, chopped
1 ½ tsp Kushi Spice (see page 23) (use 3 tsp Kushi Spice, if you're using prawns as a base meat)
½ tsp chilli powder
2 tsp sugar
Juice of half a lemon
50 ml of pre-cooked dhal (see page 34)
1 slice of pineapple (cut into chunks of you prefer)
A ladle of base "meat" (see page 17)
A ladle of base sauce (see page 15)
Fresh coriander leaves to garnish

Heat the vegetable oil in a Balti bowl, and fry the garlic until light brown.

Next, add the onion, and fry until light brown. Take off the heat.

Add the "Kushi Spice", chilli powder, sugar and lemon juice, and give it a really good mix.

Return to a very low heat, for ½ minute, stirring constantly - making sure the spices don't burn.

Add the cooked dhal followed by the pineapple and mix.

Spoon in the base 'meat' and base sauce, then stir. Simmer for two or three minutes, and it'll begin sizzling.

Garnish with fresh coriander leaves, and serve immediately. This particular dish is great with freshly cooked pilau rice. (see page 58)

See page 26 for photographs of the various stages of cooking Dhansak.

Simple dhal recipe (for use in Dhansak)

Dhal is a soup-like dish made from lentils, which is very popular with vegetarians as a main meal or side dish, and is often eaten with a chapatti or freshly cooked naan bread. As a meal in itself, it's traditionally served in a deep plate or a soup bowl - but isn't usually made or presented in a Balti bowl, as it's not a traditional Balti meal.

If you're put off by the thought of eating pulses (they do tend to have the image of a rather dull food) then please don't be. They add a unique texture and creaminess to a Balti dish, which most people are often pleasantly surprised by.

250g cup of yellow dhal / lentils (uncooked)
1200 ml (2 pints) hot (but not boiling) water
Half a medium onion, finely chopped
½ tsp salt
4 bay leaves
3 star anise
3 pieces of cinnamon stick
1 ½ tsp turmeric powder
¼ tsp coriander powder
½ tsp chilli powder

First, wash the uncooked dhal very thoroughly.

> **It's best to pour it into a saucepan, cover it with water, and then "massage" it with your hands, to get rid of any residues. Repeat this three or four times, to make sure that it's thoroughly cleaned. Sieve between washes.**

Once washed, leave the dhal in the 1200 ml of hot water for 15-20 minutes - it'll start to absorb the liquid and become softer.

Put the lentils and water into a saucepan and add the remaining ingredients. Then boil for 25-30 minutes, stirring frequently. The pulses will soften and the whole thing will form a thick liquid, rather like a soup.

> **Watch out while stirring. It has a tendency to bubble and spit and can leave nasty burns and, because it's sticky, it's a bit like molten lava!**

Once it's thickened and is soup-like, turn the heat right down, and gently simmer for a further 5-10 minutes until it's quite thick.

Once you remove the star anise, cinnamon and bay leaves, the simple dhal is ready and can be served as a main meal or used in a Balti Dhansak.

Chapter Six

Speciality curries

This chapter takes Balti cooking to a new dimension. It contains a more "in-depth" cooking method, and shows how to make two of the speciality dishes of my restaurant, including Chicken Tikka Masala which is such a popular dish in Britain that it really *has* to be included in this book.

Most restaurants will have variations on the same theme when it comes to 'speciality dishes', so the recipes in this chapter are the ones I have found that my customers prefer.

If you've enjoyed making the dishes on previous pages, I'm sure you'll find this chapter a fascinating insight into more elaborate curry cooking. You'll need to prepare two new ingredients: Masala Sauce (see page 36) and cooked chicken or lamb tikka (see page 52). As with the previous curries, it'll all come together at the end, producing a Balti to rival your local take-away.

The extra preparation takes more than an hour, as it's slightly more complicated than the previous dishes, but once you've mastered the basic Balti, these techniques should come naturally. Also, remember that the chefs who prepare these curries in restaurants have had many years of practice - so don't expect yours to be perfect first time, but as with all the other recipes - have fun!

 Each recipe in this section uses a quantity of the base sauce (see page 15). Make sure you've got enough before starting! You'll also need some Kushi Spice (see page 23). It doesn't need pre-cooked meat as before - because it uses cooked Chicken or Lamb Tikka (page 52).

Once you've made either of these two dishes, you'll see how easy it is to adapt the recipes with other ingredients, so you can experiment and create your very own signature dish.

 I really don't recommend that you try to make these dishes unless you've made the basic Balti curry in chapter 4. The techniques and understanding you gain from that chapter are invaluable in making these dishes. I also strongly recommend that you read through the recipes before attempting them to give you an idea of what additional components you'll need.

Masala Sauce

This is a thick and strong-tasting sauce, which when added to other ingredients, gives a creamy texture to speciality dishes. Like the base sauce in chapter three, it shouldn't be eaten by itself, and every restaurant has its own secret blend - this is my version.

You'll notice that food colouring is among the ingredients. The reason many restaurants still chose to include it, is simply because customers expect dishes like Chicken Tikka Masala to be quite highly coloured. In my restaurant however, I keep the levels of colouring to an absolute minimum (well within safe guidelines) and have made them optional in these recipes so you can decide whether to use them or not.

 The initial quantity of tomato sounds like a huge amount but, because it's boiled for 45 minutes or more, it reduces to a thick sauce. WARNING! Making this sauce is a test of your patience! It has to be stirred almost constantly for about an hour to prevent it from burning.

For 4-5 portions:

1250g peeled chopped tomatoes, tinned
90ml (3 fl oz) fresh single cream
½ kg sugar
100ml bottle Kewra water (available from most Asian shops)
1 tbsp garlic paste
1½ tsp ginger paste
1½ tbsp Kashmir Masala paste (normally sold in jars)
2 tbsp concentrated mint sauce
2 tbsp English mustard (not powdered)
1 tsp almond oil

2½ tbsp ground almond powder
4 tbsp coconut powder (Note this is not desiccated coconut, but a powder with a flour-like texture)
200ml tin of coconut milk
pinch of red colour powder (less than ¼ tsp) - optional
pinch of yellow colour powder (less than ¼ tsp) - optional
½ tsp chilli powder
1¼ tsp turmeric powder
½ tsp cumin powder
1 tsp coriander powder
1 tsp curry powder
¼ tsp ajowan powder
½ tsp pomegranate seed (anardana)
¼ tsp ground black cardamom
¼ tsp ground green cardamom
¼ tsp ground cinnamon
½ tsp ground cloves
¼ tsp ground black pepper

Put all the ingredients into a large saucepan (a large pressure-cooker size should do), and put on a moderate heat, stirring constantly until it starts to boil.

 It's vital that you watch the mixture all the time as the combination of ingredients (particularly the coconut, almond and spices) can easily burn and ruin the taste. Be prepared for the fact it may look bright pink at one stage. This is normal - and won't last.
Be careful! This hot mixture is very thick and can spit. It's been known to cause some nasty burns!

Turn the heat down, and simmer for 45 minutes to one hour, stirring constantly.

Finally, liquidise in a blender to make a thick red sauce, ready for use in your speciality dishes. As this contains cream and almond milk - we don't recommend freezing it.

Balti Chicken Tikka Masala

This needs no introduction whatsoever, so we'll get straight on with the recipe.

Per portion:

½ tsp vegetable oil
1 tsp ghee
1 tsp mustard seeds
2 garlic cloves, chopped - optional
One portion cooked Chicken Tikka (see page 52)
1 tsp Kushi Spice (see page 23)
Pinch of salt
1 tsp almond powder
1 tsp coconut powder (not desiccated - this powder has a flour-like texture)
1 tsp sugar
1 tsp English mustard (not powdered)
5 tbsp Masala Sauce (see page 36)
A ladle of base sauce (see page 15)
Fresh cream and coriander leaves to serve

Heat the oil and ghee in a Balti bowl.
Add the mustard seeds (which will start to pop), and then the garlic - if using. Reduce the heat, and add the cooked chicken tikka, Kushi Spice, salt, almond and coconut powder. Stir well.
Add the sugar and English mustard.
Spoon in the Masala Sauce, and a ladle of base sauce.
Increase the heat, and cook for 2-3 minutes until the chicken is warmed through and the sauce is bubbling.
Stir in 1 teaspoon of cream, and finish the dish with a swirl of cream and a sprinkle of fresh coriander leaves. Serve.

Chicken Tikka Masala goes well with more or less any accompaniment - breads or rices.

Balti Chicken Tikka Shashlik Masala

This is a variation on Balti Chicken Tikka Masala (see page 37), and has one of the longest names of any restaurant curry. It's a rich dish, spiced up with a generous amount of fresh onion, pepper and mushroom, and uses a slightly different amount of the Masala Sauce. This dish will give you an idea of how Masala Sauce affects the taste, so you can experiment further when creating your own speciality curries.

Per portion:

1 tsp vegetable oil
2-3 tsp ghee
1 garlic clove, crushed or chopped
1 medium sized onion, cut into 1 cm strips
¼ green pepper, chopped
½ tsp mustard seeds
2 mushrooms, sliced (cooked or uncooked)
1½ tsp Kushi Spice (see page 23)
Pinch of salt
1½ tsp sugar
1½ tsp almond powder
1 tsp coconut powder (not desiccated - this powder has a flour-like texture)
6-7 tbsp Masala Sauce (see page 36)
1 portion of cooked Chicken Tikka (see page 52)
1 ladle of base sauce (see page 15)
Fresh cream and fresh coriander leaves to garnish

Put the Balti bowl on the heat, and add the vegetable oil and ghee.

Fry the garlic for about 30 seconds.

Add the onion, green pepper, and mustard seeds (which will pop slightly) - and stir until it begins to brown.

Next, add the mushrooms. (If you're using uncooked mushrooms, stir this mixture for a minute of so until they soften.)

Reduce the heat, and add the Kushi Spice, salt, sugar, almond powder and coconut powder.

Mix thoroughly, then add the Masala Sauce, followed by the cooked Chicken Tikka, and the base sauce. Heat for for 3-4 minutes until the chicken is warm throughout and the sauce is bubbling.

Garnish with a swirl of fresh cream and a touch of coriander leaves, and serve.

 As you can appreciate, there are literally dozens of variations on these speciality curries, using many different ingredients. You can use pre-cooked lamb tikka or vegetables, and add more or less whatever you want to the curry. I hope that by making these dishes, you'll have the confidence to experiment further, and tailor them to include your favourite ingredients.

Chapter Seven

Other interesting dishes

Certain dishes don't really fit into the categories covered in previous chapters, and so get a section of their own.

All these recipes build on the techniques from the Basic Balti on page 25, and are easier than the Balti Chicken Tikka Masala (and no more difficult than a Rogan Josh) to master.

Please read through the recipe you are cooking to make sure you have enough base sauce, base "meat" or Kushi Spice, where required, and check the portion sizes as some of these dishes - which can be served as starters or main courses - may serve more than one.

I have included the delicious Chicken Korma (which is one of the most popular dishes among people who don't like their curry too spicy) in this section, rather than any other, because it requires a slightly different base sauce. It also shows how different techniques can be used to produce a completely different end-product.

Also included is the exotic King Prawn Sagwala, which shows the technique for dealing with shellfish.

No curry cookbook would be complete without the fabulous Bombay Potato - also known as Bombay Aloo. A spicy vegetable dish - served as a main course or accompaniment.

Chicken Korma Base Sauce

Chicken Korma is a mild, fragrant dish made with coconut. Many people who are new to curry cuisine choose this in restaurants, and it always goes down well. It has a different taste to many of the curries we've made before because it uses an alternative version of the base sauce, which doesn't include the powdered spice and tomato. The techniques here will be quite familiar, as they're similar to the base sauce on page 15.

 You'll need Kushi Spice in the completed dish, and a portion of pre-cooked chicken (see page 18).

For 2-3 portions:

3 large onions (approx 600g), chopped
1 tsp salt
3 carrots, chopped
1 fresh red pepper, diced
1 fresh green pepper, diced

1050ml (1¾ pints) water

2 star anise
2 cloves
3 pieces of cinnamon stick
4 bay leaves
2-3 cardamom pods

Put the onions, salt, carrots, peppers and water into a good sized saucepan.

Place all the whole spices into a clean piece of net (as with the original base sauce) and drop into the pan.

Boil for around 20 minutes on a high heat - then reduce the heat, cover and simmer for another five minutes.

Remove the net containing the spices and throw it away.

Allow to cool, and blend to a smooth sauce using a liquidiser.

Chicken Korma recipe

Once the Korma base sauce (see page 40) has been made, you can make the dish itself.

Per portion:

2 tbsp vegetable oil
2 tbsp ghee (clarified butter)
4 garlic cloves, crushed
1 ladle of pre-cooked chicken (see page 18)
2 tsp almond powder
2-3 tsp coconut powder (not desiccated)
1 tsp sugar
80 ml coconut milk
8-10 sultanas
2 tsp Kushi Spice (see page 23)
80 ml fresh milk
1 ladle Chicken Korma base sauce (see page 40)

Heat the Balti bowl, adding the vegetable oil and ghee.

Gently brown the garlic, and add a portion of pre-cooked chicken.

Stir for around a minute on a low heat.

Then add the almond powder, coconut powder, sugar, coconut milk, sultanas and Kushi Spice.

Stir this continuously, for about a minute. This mixture is very prone to burning if not stirred constantly.

Then add the fresh milk, followed by a ladle of the Chicken Korma base sauce, again, stirring frequently.

Simmer for three minutes, or until it becomes the desired thickness, and serve.

Best served with plain basmati rice.

Bombay Potato (Bombay Aloo)

A hot and slightly dry dish (meaning it's not swimming in sauce - but still moist in texture) which can be served as a side dish or a main course. It includes chunks of potato, coated in a flavoursome mixture of spices and is best served with a paratha or chapatti.

Makes about 3 portions as a side dish. About 2 portions as a main meal:

6 medium potatoes, peeled and cut into 1 inch cubes
3 tbsp vegetable oil
6 garlic cloves, chopped
1 large onion, roughly chopped
1 tsp cumin seeds
2 green chillies, finely chopped (Leave the seeds in)
1 tsp chilli powder
2 tsp Kushi Spice (see page 23)
½ ladle base sauce (see page 15)
1 tomato, diced
Fresh coriander leaves to garnish

Boil the potatoes for about five minutes (so they're slightly cooked, but not liable to fall apart) then rinse in cold water, drain in a colander, and put to one side.

Heat the vegetable oil in a large frying pan or wok, and fry the garlic until it starts to brown.

Add the onion and cook until it starts to soften.

Then add the cumin seeds, stirring constantly, followed by the chillies.

Reduce the heat, add the chilli powder and Kushi Spice, stirring constantly (so the spices don't burn) for about 1 minute.

Then add about a half a cupful of hot water, and bring to the boil.

Continue to boil for about two minutes, stirring constantly.

Then add the potato, and base sauce.

Stir gently - making sure you don't break the potato.

Add the tomato, and cook for a few more minutes.

Sprinkle generously with fresh coriander leaves, and slightly mix it into the dish by giving it a gentle stir. Serve.

Chana (Chick Pea) Chat

Chana Chat is a vegetarian dish made with succulent chick peas, cucumber, ginger, garlic and a fragrant mixture of spices called Chat Masala. It appeals particularly to children, and can be served as a starter or main course. I recommend serving this with a green salad, garnished with tomato, cucumber and drizzled with olive oil.

For 2-3 portions:

2 tbsp vegetable oil
4 garlic cloves, finely chopped + 1 garlic clove, finely sliced
1 medium onion, finely diced
½ green pepper, chopped
½ red pepper, chopped
2 green chillies, chopped
1 tomato, diced
400g tin of cooked chick peas, drained
3 tsp Kushi Spice (see page 23)
2 tsp chat masala powder (easily available from speciality shops)
1½ tsp chopped ginger
¼ cucumber, finely chopped
Juice of half a lemon
Fresh coriander leaves to garnish

Heat the vegetable oil in a large saucepan.

Add the chopped garlic, and cook until golden brown.

Next, add the onion and pepper, and fry for a few minutes until it softens.

Add the chillies, tomato and chick peas. Stir well.

Turn the heat down, add the Kushi Spice and chat masala powder - stirring constantly so the spices don't burn.

Add the sliced garlic, followed by the ginger, and cook for one minute.

Then add the cucumber, which will start to sweat down, releasing water. Cook for a minute or so before adding the lemon juice and coriander leaves to garnish.

King Prawn Sagwala

A must for prawn lovers everywhere. Quite expensive - but definitely worth it - and made all the more interesting by the addition of spinach which brings a unique flavour to Balti cookery. This dish is best served with rice.

Per portion:

200g fresh king prawns
100g fresh spinach, washed
4 tsp vegetable oil
½ tsp mustard seeds
2-3 garlic cloves, finely sliced
2-3 pieces of cinnamon stick (each 2-3 inches long)
3 green cardamom pods
4 bay leaves
8 cloves
1 onion, finely chopped
4 green chilli peppers, chopped
½ red pepper, diced
½ tsp salt
6 tsp Kushi Spice (see page 23)
½ tsp turmeric powder
¼ tsp cumin powder
1 ladle of base sauce (see page 15)
1 whole tomato, cubed
Handful of fresh coriander leaves

First, prepare the king prawns. Remove the shell by slitting lengthways along the middle and remove the black vein running along the length of the prawn. (If you need help, your fishmonger should be able to show you.) Cut each into four pieces.

Next, take the spinach, chop the leaves roughly and steam them for 2-3 minutes until they soften and reduce quite dramatically in size.

 If you don't have a steamer, take a small colander and rest it on top of a saucepan of boiling water.

Heat the vegetable oil in a Balti bowl, and then add the mustard seeds, garlic, cinnamon, cardamom, bay leaves and cloves - stirring constantly for about a minute.

Then add the fresh king prawns, which will become pink as they cook.
Stir for about 3 minutes, before adding the onion, chillies, pepper and salt. Continue stirring for about two minutes, and reduce the heat, before adding the Kushi Spice, turmeric and cumin. Stir constantly.
Then add the spinach and base sauce, and cook for a further 2-3 minutes.

Add the tomato, and cook for a minute, stirring well, before garnishing with fresh coriander leaves. Serve.

 You can leave the cinnamon, bay leaves, cardamom and cloves in the completed dish - but feel free to remove them if you don't like the texture.

Aloo Mushroom

Aloo Mushroom is quite a dry dish as it only uses half a ladle of base sauce. It's great as a snack or a main meal and goes particularly well with all sorts of bread. I have actually tried this with normal sliced bread from the supermarket - and was pleasantly surprised with the result! That's not the sort of thing you'd expect a restaurateur to say - but give it a go.

Makes about 3 portions as a side dish. About 2 portions as a main meal:

4 medium potatoes, cut into 1 inch cubes
1 tbsp vegetable oil
5 garlic cloves, crushed or chopped finely
1 medium onion, finely chopped
4 tsp Kushi Spice (see page 23)
200g fresh mushrooms, quartered
½ ladle of base sauce (see page 15)
½ red pepper, chopped finely
2 green chillies, chopped
Half a tomato
Fresh coriander leaves to garnish

Boil the potatoes in unsalted water for around five minutes, then drain.

Place a large Balti bowl or wok onto a moderate heat.

Add the vegetable oil, and the garlic until it starts to brown.

Add the onion and let that brown too.

Remove from the heat and add the Kushi Spice - stirring well.

Continue to stir and then add the mushroom.

Return to a low heat and allow to "sweat" for 30 seconds.

Add the potato and base sauce then stir well - making sure you don't break the potato.

Heat for about a minute before adding the tomato, chillies and peppers.

Cover if possible and cook for 4-5 minutes.

Garnish with fresh coriander leaves, mix slightly, and heat through for a further 30 seconds.

Gobi Mushroom

This is a similar dish to Aloo Mushroom (see page 45) but uses cauliflower instead of potato.

Serves 2 as a main course. 3 as a starter or side dish:

1½ tbsp vegetable oil
3 garlic cloves, sliced
1 small onion, finely chopped
2½ tsp Kushi Spice (see page 23)
½ fresh medium cauliflower (about 160g), cut into florets
100ml water
200g fresh mushrooms, quartered
2 tomatoes, chopped
2 green chilli, finely chopped
¼ green pepper, chopped
¼ red pepper, chopped
Fresh coriander leaves to garnish
A quantity of base sauce (optional - see below)

Heat the vegetable oil in a wok or large saucepan.

Add the garlic and onion and fry until golden brown.

Remove from the heat and add the Kushi Spice.

Add the (raw) cauliflower then the water. Stir well and return to the heat.

Cover if possible, and simmer for 3 minutes, stirring regularly.

Add the mushroom, re-cover and continue cooking for another minute.

Add the tomato, chillies and peppers. Mix well and simmer for 3 minutes.

Add a handful of fresh coriander leaves and simmer for a further two minutes. Serve.

 You may notice that this recipe doesn't contain any base sauce. It doesn't really need it because the cauliflower and mushrooms release liquid during the cooking process. If you add some towards the end of the recipe, it gives the curry a slightly different texture. I recommend you try both, so you can decide which you prefer.

Mutter Panneer

Mutter Panneer is a traditional dish among South Indian people - especially in the Madras area. I learned this method from a South Indian chef I worked with in London and it's very different to any other curry recipe in this book. An interesting combination - consisting of a spicy mixture of cheese and peas - and something of an acquired taste.

 Panneer cheese is widely available from Indian shops, and is now being stocked by some supermarkets.

For 3-4 portions:

2 tbsp vegetable oil
250g panneer cheese, cut into 1 cm cubes
5 tsp ghee
6-8 garlic cloves, chopped
1 onion, finely chopped
½ inch of ginger, shredded
175g peas
¼ tsp cumin seed
6 tsp Kushi Spice (see page 23) This sounds like a lot of spice - but it makes up for the creaminess of the cheese - and the lack of any strong flavour in the peas
½ green pepper, chopped
½ red pepper, chopped
4 green chillies, chopped
Half a tomato, chopped
Slice of lemon
Handful of fresh coriander leaves

Heat the vegetable oil in a frying pan until very hot, and fry the panneer until the pieces become golden brown.

Pour into a bowl, and add cold water to immediately cool the panneer. Drain, and set to one side.

Clean the frying pan, then return to the heat and add 4 teaspoons of ghee. (Keep 1 teaspoon of ghee back to garnish.)

Fry the garlic, onion and ginger until light brown.

Add the peas, and cook for about 2 minutes until they start to become coloured.

Remove from the heat, and add the cumin seed and Kushi Spice.

Continue to stir as you return it to a low heat for a minute.

Then add the panneer, green and red peppers, chilli peppers, tomato and slice of lemon.

Cover if possible, and cook for around three minutes - the mixture will soften and combine.

Stir, add the coriander leaves to garnish, pour over 1 tsp of ghee and serve. It's traditional to leave the lemon in the dish.

Chapter Eight

Starters, breads and accompaniments

Starters, accompaniments and Indian snacks are already becoming familiar sights on the shelves of most supermarkets and, to give them credit, some of them aren't too bad. But, there's nothing like a freshly prepared onion bhaji or an exotic lamb or chicken kebab, sprinkled with fresh coriander. They just have that extra "something" which you simply don't get from the pre-packaged variety, plus they're really easy to make and can be prepared in advance of your Balti curry dinner party.

This chapter also contains recipes for some of the side dishes, traditionally served with Balti meals.

For that real restaurant experience, serve the starters with a crisp salad and either a cooling mint sauce (see page 49) or a fiery lime pickle.

Starters

Breads and accompaniments

Mint Sauce

Very easy to make, this is the ideal accompaniment to a variety of starters. Served straight from the fridge, it has a fresh taste which counteracts the spiciness of any food it's served with.

 Many restaurants will give a complementary portion of this sauce with popadoms, along with spiced onions and chutneys.

For 6 portions:

1 garlic clove
¼ tsp crushed fresh ginger
1 tbsp mustard oil (This may be difficult to find in supermarkets - but is widely available in Asian shops)
2 tbsp sugar
Pinch of salt
¼ tsp coriander powder
¼ tsp cumin powder
2 tsp concentrated mint sauce - as bought from a supermarket
400g tub of natural yoghurt

Place all the ingredients (except the yoghurt) into a blender and mix thoroughly.

Pour into a bowl, add the yoghurt and mix well. Refrigerate if not serving immediately.

Cool mint sauce - delicious with popadoms.

Onion Bhaji

The classic starter for any meal in a curry house. Shredded onion is mixed with a spicy batter, and deep fried until golden. Best served with Mint Sauce (page 49), and a crisp green salad. Some restaurants - particularly in Birmingham's Balti Belt - even offer free onion bhajis with main meals as an incentive to attract more customers.

For 4-6 portions:

500g onion, quartered, and chopped into slices.
1 ½ tsp chilli powder
1 tsp turmeric powder
½ tsp cumin powder
1 ½ tsp coriander powder
1 tbsp coriander seeds
250g "gram flour" (available from Asian shops and some supermarkets)

Dry roast the coriander seeds in a frying pan with no oil until they've finished popping.

Add the spices and coriander seeds to the onion, and mix very well with your hands - giving it a good "massage". Allow to rest for five minutes. The onions will start to release a small amount of liquid.

Then add the gram flour and 150 ml of cold water, and mix until it takes on a semi dry consistency (like a thick batter) which you can shape with your hands.

 Plain flour won't work won't work for this recipe, as it doesn't give the right consistency and flavour.

Take a handful of the mixture and make into a ball shape (slightly bigger than a billiard ball) in your palm. If it falls apart easily, you'll need more flour.

Gently lower this into a deep fat fryer at a temperature specified by the manufacturer - about 170 degrees is usually adequate. You can make several bhajis at a time.

Once this has started cooking, turn the heat up slightly to about 200 degrees.

Cook for about eight minutes, then take one out and test it by sticking a fork in. If the fork comes out clean, then it's ready.

 It's best to experiment before your Balti dinner party, as there's a knack to making the perfect bhaji. They can be made up to three days in advance and kept in the fridge, but the raw "batter-and-onion" mixture does not keep well. To reheat, place in the microwave for about 30 seconds each, and deep fry for a minute or two to make them as good as new.

Pakora

Delicious served with a traditional mint sauce (see page 49) and a selection of chutneys, pakora is a slight variation on the onion bhaji theme. It has a slightly different taste because it's made of smaller pieces and also contains potato.

For 6-8 portions:

500g onion, coarsely diced
125g potato, cut into ¾ cm cubes
1 ½ tsp chilli powder
½ tsp turmeric powder
¾ tsp cumin powder
1 ½ tsp coriander powder
1 tbsp each of coriander seeds and fenugreek seeds
250g "gram flour" (available from Asian shops and some supermarkets)

Thoroughly mix the spices, onion and potato using your hands - giving them a good "massage". Leave this for five minutes. The onions will start to release a small amount of liquid.

Then add the gram flour and 150 ml of cold water. Plain flour won't work won't work for this recipe, as it doesn't give the right consistency and flavour. Again, mix well.

The mixture will take on a semi dry consistency like a thick batter, which you can shape with your hands.

Pick up small piece (about the size of a golf ball) and lower gently into a deep fat fryer at a temperature specified by the manufacturer - about 170 degrees. Repeat with several more pieces.

Turn the heat up slightly to about 200 degrees.

Fry for about five minutes, until cooked through and not sticky to the touch.

Chicken / Lamb Tikka

This is a dry starter, which can also be used in other recipes like the famous Chicken Tikka Masala. It's simply chunks of lamb or chicken marinated in a mixture of spices and yoghurt, which gives the meat a wonderful flavour and texture, and then cooked in a tandoori oven. (For the purposes of cooking at home, a grill works just as well.)

The "dryness" is complimented beautifully with some mint sauce (see page 49), mango chutney or lime pickle, and it's a particularly good starter for anyone new to Indian cuisine.

For 6-8 chicken breasts or lamb fillets (enough for a few starters, and some left over to make Tikka Masala):

4 tsp garlic paste
5½ tsp ginger paste
5 tbsp mustard oil
6 tsp Kashmir Masala paste
Juice of 1 lemon
6 tsp mint sauce (concentrated)
3 tsp mustard (not powdered)
a pinch each of red and yellow food colouring powder (optional)
220g plain yoghurt
½ tsp chilli powder (more if you like it hotter)
2 tsp turmeric powder
1 tsp cumin powder
3 tsp coriander powder
2 tsp curry powder
2½ tsp garam masala powder
2 tsp dried fenugreek leaves, chopped

First, you'll need to make a marinade for the meat by mixing the ingredients in a large bowl to give a smooth sauce with no lumps.

 This marinade can be kept in the fridge for several days if you're not using it all.

Then, choose your meat - chicken breasts or lamb fillets. (Keep these whole - as we'll cut them up into the more familiar bite-sized tikka pieces at the end.)

Really mix the meat into the marinade, massaging it for a few minutes with your hands, to work the spices into the fillets. It's important that all the surface of the meat is covered. Sprinkle a few pinches of fresh chopped coriander leaves onto this mixture, and cover with cling film. Refrigerate for 24 hours.

When it's time to cook, preheat the grill to a medium heat. Put the meat onto metal skewers to make them easier to handle, and place under the grill for about three minutes. Turn them over, and cook for a further three minutes. Keep doing this until they're cooked thoroughly, which may take up to a quarter of an hour depending on the thickness of the chicken and the power of your grill.

Cut a piece in half to make sure it's thoroughly cooked, then cut into bite-sized chunks, and serve

Chicken / Lamb Shashlik

This starter is served on skewers and uses the popular chicken or lamb tikka (see page 52), with vegetables and onions.

Follow the same marinating process as the tikka recipe on the previous page, **except cut the meat into inch-sized cubes before cooking.**

Once it's marinated, the procedure for shashlik begins to differ from that of plain tikka.

Put the meat onto the skewers but separate each piece alternately with onion, green pepper, red pepper, mushroom, sliced courgette - or whatever vegetables you want.

Preheat the grill to a medium heat. Put the skewers under the grill for about a minute, then rotate through 90 degrees, and cook on each "side" for 2 minutes each. (The time it takes can vary depending on the temperature of your grill.)

Test the meat with a fork or catering thermometer to make sure it's cooked. As a rule, if it feels springy, it's not ready yet and needs more cooking time. Cut a chunk in half to make sure.

Remove from the grill and serve.

Sheekh Kebab

Made from minced lamb, this starter also contains green chillies, coriander, ginger, garlic, herbs and spices. It's traditionally cooked on skewers in a charcoal oven, but still tastes great when cooked under the grill.

For 5 portions (10 kebabs):

450g minced lamb
1 tsp garlic paste
¾ tsp ginger paste
1½ tsp Kushi Spice (see page 23)
1½ tsp Kashmir Masala paste
A generous pinch of fresh coriander leaves, chopped finely
8 whole green chillies, finely chopped

Put all the ingredients into a bowl and mix very thoroughly - making sure the spice is evenly spread throughout.

 You'll need quite thick skewers - about ½ cm in diameter - most catering shops will know what you want if you tell them what you're making.

Wrap a good handful of the mixture around each of the skewers forming a sausage shape that's about 15 cm long.

Pre-heat the grill to a high heat. Put the kebabs under the grill for two to three minutes - turning every minute until they're cooked. Once cooked, hold the kebab with a clean cloth, and pull from the skewer.

Kushi Kebab

This is a Kushi Balti House speciality. Most restaurants will have a variation of it, but this is the recipe which, I feel, gives the best results. It's a similar idea to the sheekh kebab (page 53), but rather than being cooked on a skewer, it's shaped into a flat patty and fried. I describe it on my menu as "Lamb mince mixed with whole coriander, fresh herbs and spices and fried".

For 4 portions (4 kebabs):

450g minced lamb
1 ½ tsp garlic paste
1 ½ tsp ginger paste
1 ¾ tsp Kushi Spice (see page 23)
1 ¼ tsp Kashmir Masala paste
1 tsp whole coriander seeds
½ tsp fenugreek seeds
¼ tsp shahi jeera seeds - if available
A generous pinch of fresh coriander leaves, chopped finely

Place all the ingredients into a bowl and mix thoroughly with your hands, making sure the spice is evenly spread throughout.

Take about a quarter of the mixture and use the palms of your hands to shape into a flat oval-shaped patty which is no more than 1 cm thick.

Take a frying pan and brush with vegetable oil. Put on a medium heat.

Add the kebabs to the pan. (There's only really room for two at a time.)

Heat the pan gently, and cook the kebabs for about four minutes per side

 Hold the pan at a slight angle so you can drain away any large amounts of liquid and fat that are produced during the cooking process. (If you let it sit in its own fat, it'll turn out like a hamburger.)

When the kebab takes on a firm texture, it's ready. Check it's cooked through properly before serving.

Breads

Naan bread is the traditional accompaniment in Indian and Bangladeshi restaurants. Unfortunately, these are very difficult to prepare at home as they are made in a specialist tandoori oven, which cooks both sides of the bread at the same time. They are made of clay and produce a very high temperature which can't be achieved under a domestic grill or in the oven. I could give you a version of a Naan bread recipe but the result would be disappointing - and nowhere near as good as the Naan you'd get in a restaurant.

However, there are alternatives to the famous Naan - and in my view they're even better. So, instead of a Naan bread, why not try a chapatti or thick roti? They're slightly different, despite using the same dough mixture.

Basic dough mixture

For about 10 chapattis or 3 parathas:

500g chapatti flour (available from Asian shops and some supermarkets)
Approximately 250ml water (the amount varies - see below)
Pinch of salt

Put the flour into a good-sized bowl, add around a cup of the water, and mix well with your hands.

Now, add the pinch of salt and keep mixing in small amounts of water, until the dough becomes the consistency of pastry - as if you're making an apple pie.

 It's impossible to say exactly how much water you'll need, as this varies greatly with the brand of flour you're using - and even atmospheric humidity!

Finally, knead well for a few minutes then wrap with cling film, leaving it on a work surface at room temperature for at least 30 to 45 minutes to relax.

Chapatti

A chapatti is quite thin. If you prefer a thicker and more fluffy bread, try the roti below. Again, a tandoori oven is really needed here - but these two breads produce decent results when made at home.

Basic dough mixture (see page 55)
Chapatti flour for sprinkling

Take a golf-ball sized amount (about 60g) of the dough mixture, and put onto a lightly floured surface.

Roll this out with a rolling pin until it's as thin as you can make it, without it breaking or sticking to the surface.

Put this into a **dry** frying pan on a high heat. Cook on one side until you see small "blisters" appearing on the underside.

Then turn over and do the same. Your chapatti is ready to eat.

Roti

This accompaniment is more like the traditional naan bread than the chapatti.

Basic dough mixture (see page 55)
Chapatti flour for sprinkling

Roll a piece of dough to the size of a tennis ball (about 200g), and flatten with a rolling pin to make a circle of about 6 inch diameter.

Put this into a **dry** frying pan on a low heat.

Cook both sides for a couple of minutes each.

Then pinch the roti. If it feels spongy it's ready. (If it doesn't bounce back, cook it for a further minute per side until it becomes spongy.)

Paratha

Paratha is a slightly more "interesting" type of bread and involves melted butter for a richer taste. It's also good fun to make - although it takes a bit more preparation than the previous recipes for chapatti and roti.

Basic dough mixture (see page 55)
Melted butter
Chapatti flour for sprinkling

Take a tennis ball sized portion of dough (about 200g) and place onto a lightly floured surface.

Roll into a flat circle of about 12 -16 inches diameter using a rolling pin. (This will be bigger and flatter than the completed paratha.)

Brush melted butter onto one side of the dough, sprinkle a pinch of chapatti flour evenly onto the buttered side, then roll the whole thing into a long "sausage" - rather like a swiss roll. ▶

Then roll this around on itself - into a spiral. ▶

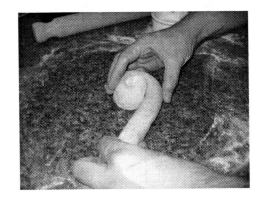

Flatten with a rolling pin until it's about 8 inches in diameter.

Very carefully, lift the paratha from the work surface and put into a **dry** frying pan over a high heat.

Cook both sides for a couple of minutes each.

Remove the paratha, then clean the pan with a piece of kitchen roll.

Finally add two teaspoons of melted butter to the pan, put the paratha back, and cook for a minute or two. Turn over and cook for another minute. Serve.

Pilau Rice

Pilau rice is the classic side order. In restaurants, we serve tonnes and tonnes of it every year, and many of my customers ask me what is the best way to cook the perfect pilau. It's very easy - and all in the preparation.

In many restaurants, you may have seen that pilau rice has mainly white grains, but some are coloured orange and yellow. If you want this effect, you can use saffron as a natural colour - but you'll need to start this before you cook the rice. The instructions for this are highlighted in *italics* within the recipe.

For 4-5 portions:

2 cups of good uncooked basmati rice. (Approx 500g)

2 tbsp vegetable oil
5 bay leaves
3 cardamom pods
3 cinnamon sticks (each 2-3 inches long)
3 star anise
¼ tsp salt
¼ tsp fenugreek seeds
¼ tsp of shahi jeera seeds - if available
Saffron (optional - for colouring)

Put the rice into a large bowl, and wash thoroughly with warm water three of four times - sieving between washes. Once it's thoroughly cleaned, drain in a sieve, and put to one side.

 Give the rice a good massage with your hands, to get rid of any grease or starch.

Put a generous pinch of saffron into a teacup, add a dash of boiling water, and leave it to soften and "brew". (Keep the same quantity of dry saffron to one side.)

Put two cups of hot - but not boiling - water into a large saucepan, along with the rest of the ingredients.

Finally, add the rice, and bring to the boil.

Boil until the water just covers the rice, giving a good stir every now and then to make sure it doesn't stick to the bottom of the saucepan.

Add the saffron mixture, putting the liquid on one side of the pan, and the dry saffron on the other.

Reduce the heat to very very low, cover and continue to cook for 15 to 20 minutes.

Then, lift the lid, and take a small amount of rice with a spoon. Squash a few grains between your fingers (Watch out - it's hot!), and if it's soft and smooth, the rice is ready.

Drain and serve.

Index of recipes

Please see page 11 before attempting to cook any of the curries in this book.

The **www.baltibook.co.uk** website

Visit **www.baltibook.co.uk** for more recipes and additional support on how to cook the dishes in this book.

The site also contains lists of recommended suppliers and gives updated information on the recipes featured.

All services provided by the website are subject to availability and change. Terms and conditions apply.

Acknowledgments

Cover photography by Adrian Charles Photography, Yardley, Birmingham. Tel 0121 784 1555

The authors would like thank the following people for their help and assistance in the making of this book:

Haroon Akhtar, S.M. Bashir Uddin, M. Nasir, Shelyna Begum Ali, M.A. Akbar, M.A. Atther, M.A. Akram, Salmah Begum Ali, Aishah Begum Ali, Mohammed Rahmat Ali

Jo Hebdon, Joe Holmes, Lionel Johnson, Catherine Pouncett, Jon Hawkins, Jean Kelford, Simon Clarke, Martin White

Thanks also to the following companies for allowing photos to be taken on their premises:

Sonali Supermarket, Coventry Road, Birmingham

Sweet Mahal, Stratford Road, Birmingham

About the authors

Born in Bangladesh, Mohammed Ali Haydor is the head chef of the Kushi Balti Restaurant in Birmingham. He has worked as a professional chef for three decades and has travelled extensively to research the ideal Balti curry. Most recently, he was the head chef in a successful world record attempt to create the world's largest onion bhaji.

Andy Holmes is a West Midlands journalist with more than ten years experience in national, regional and local broadcasting. A self-confessed curry-holic, with a keen interest in experimental cookery, he has teamed up with Mr. Haydor to expose the secrets of Balti cooking in "Authentic Balti Curry : Restaurant Recipes Revealed".

ISBN 141205592-X